BACKYARD BIRDS

Goldfinches

by Elizabeth Neuenfeldt

BLASTOFF!
READERS

BELLWETHER MEDIA • MINNEAPOLIS, MN

Blastoff! Readers are carefully developed by literacy experts to build reading stamina and move students toward fluency by combining standards-based content with developmentally appropriate text.

Level 1 provides the most support through repetition of high-frequency words, light text, predictable sentence patterns, and strong visual support.

Level 2 offers early readers a bit more challenge through varied sentences, increased text load, and text-supportive special features.

Level 3 advances early-fluent readers toward fluency through increased text load, less reliance on photos, advancing concepts, longer sentences, and more complex special features.

★ **Blastoff! Universe**

Reading Level

Grade
K

Grades
1–3

BLASTOFF!
DISCOVERY

Grade
4

This edition first published in 2022 by Bellwether Media, Inc.

No part of this publication may be reproduced in whole or in part without written permission of the publisher. For information regarding permission, write to Bellwether Media, Inc., Attention: Permissions Department, 6012 Blue Circle Drive, Minnetonka, MN 55343.

Library of Congress Cataloging-in-Publication Data

Names: Neuenfeldt, Elizabeth, author.
Title: Goldfinches / by Elizabeth Neuenfeldt.
Description: Minneapolis, MN : Bellwether Media, 2022. | Series: Blastoff! readers : Backyard birds | Includes bibliographical references and index. | Audience: Ages 5-8 | Audience: Grades K-1 | Summary: "Developed by literacy experts for students in kindergarten through grade three, this book introduces goldfinches to young readers through leveled text and related photos"– Provided by publisher.
Identifiers: LCCN 2021000680 (print) | LCCN 2021000681 (ebook) | ISBN 9781644874936 (library binding) | ISBN 9781648344015 (ebook)
Subjects: LCSH: Goldfinches–Juvenile literature.
Classification: LCC QL696.P246 N47 2022 (print) | LCC QL696.P246 (ebook) | DDC 598.8/85–dc23
LC record available at https://lccn.loc.gov/2021000680
LC ebook record available at https://lccn.loc.gov/2021000681

Editor: Betsy Rathburn   Designer: Andrea Schneider

Printed in the United States of America, North Mankato, MN.

Table of Contents

What Are Goldfinches?

Goldfinches are tiny birds. They are in the finch family.

All in the Family

Lawrence's goldfinch

lesser goldfinch

American goldfinch

5

Females have brown, yellow, and black feathers. Males have brighter feathers than females.

male

female

7

Goldfinches live in weedy fields. They **perch** on branches in trees and bushes.

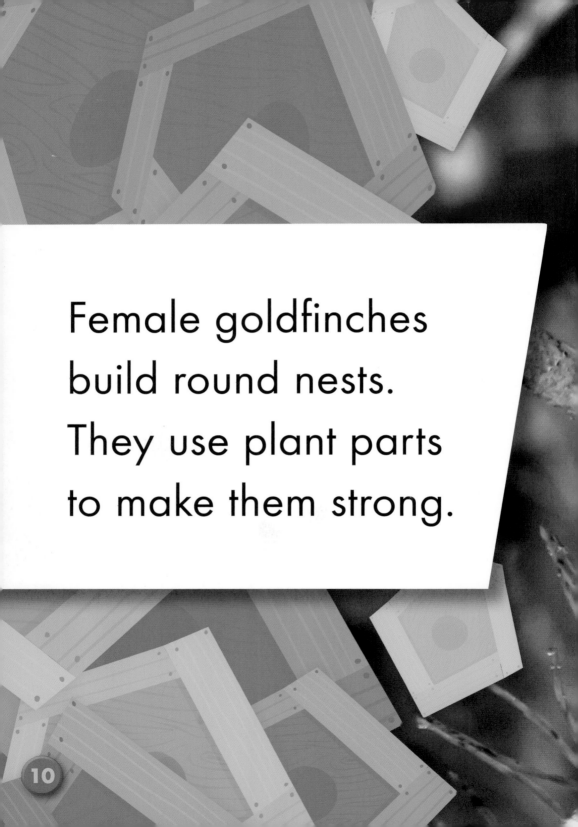

Female goldfinches
build round nests.
They use plant parts
to make them strong.

nest

Goldfinches eat seeds. They cut seeds open with their **bills**.

bill

Goldfinch Food

seeds

Goldfinches fly in **flocks**. Flocks look like they are dancing when they fly!

flock

15

Some flocks **migrate**. They fly to warmer places in winter. Other flocks stay put.

migrating

17

Goldfinches often sing while they fly. These **songbirds** have many calls!

Goldfinch Call

po-ta-to-chip!

These pretty birds stand out everywhere they go!

Glossary

bills

the mouths of birds

perch

to sit or rest on something high above the ground

flocks

groups of birds

songbirds

birds that make musical sounds

migrate

to travel with the seasons

To Learn More

AT THE LIBRARY

Neuenfeldt, Elizabeth. *Chickadees*. Minneapolis, Minn.: Bellwether Media, 2022.

Sewell, Matt. *The Atlas of Amazing Birds*. New York, N.Y.: Princeton Architectural Press, 2020.

Ward, Jennifer. *How to Find a Bird*. New York, N.Y.: Beach Lane Books, 2020.

ON THE WEB

FACTSURFER

Factsurfer.com gives you a safe, fun way to find more information.

1. Go to www.factsurfer.com.

2. Enter "goldfinches" into the search box and click 🔍.

3. Select your book cover to see a list of related content.

Index

The images in this book are reproduced through the courtesy of: Brian E Kushner, front cover (goldfinch); Viewfoto studio, front cover (background); Tathoms, p. 3; Agnieszka Bacal, pp. 4-5; William Leaman/ Alamy, p. 5 (Lawrence's goldfinch); David G Hayes, p. 5 (lesser goldfinch); Natalia Kuzmina, p. 5 (American goldfinch); Greg A Wilson, pp. 6-7; Tony Campbell, p. 7 (male); Al Mueller, pp. 8-9; Anne Richard, pp. 10-11; Danita Delimont/ Alamy, p. 11 (nest); Sergei Bolshakov, pp. 12-13; AN NGUYEN, p. 13 (seeds); Kasabutskaya Nataliya, p. 13 (weeds); Drakuliren, pp. 14-15; Danita Delimont, pp. 16-17; Nature Photographers Ltd/ Alamy, p. 17 (migrating); Gay Bumgarner/ Alamy, pp. 18-19; Matt Inman, pp. 20-21; Dave Chafin, p. 22 (bills); Ballygally View Images, p. 22 (flocks); Digoarpi, p. 22 (migrate); rck_953, p. 22 (perch); Max Allen/ Alamy, p. 22 (songbirds); Mike Truchon, p. 23.